Playtime

Jennifer Bové

muddy boots™

we jump in puddles

Guilford, Connecticut

Published by Muddy Boots
An imprint of Globe Pequot
MuddyBootsBooks.com

Distributed by NATIONAL BOOK NETWORK

The National Wildlife Federation © 2017 All rights reserved

Book design by Katie Jennings Design

Front cover photo © Getty Images/Anup Shah, back cover photo and page 8 © iStock/Anagramm, title page and page 13 © Getty Images/Johnny Johnson, table of contents and page 14 © Getty Images/Janette Hill/robertharding, page 2 © Getty Images/Jim Kruger, page 3 © Getty Images/caizier, page 5 © John Rollins, page 6 © Getty Images/Richard Du Toit/Minden Pictures, page 9 © Getty Images/Mats Lindberg, page 10 © Getty Images/W. Wayne Lockwood, M.D./Corbis/VCG, page 11 © Getty Images/Danita Delimont, page 16 © Getty Images/Daryl Balfour, page 18 © Getty Images/Anup Shah, page 19 © Getty Images/Konrad Wothe, page 20 © Getty Images/George Clerk, page 21 © Getty Images/Paul Souders, page 22 © Getty Images/PeskyMonkey, page 23 © Getty Images/Pete Oxford, page 24 © Getty Images/Jeremy Richards, page 26 © iStock/Louise Cunningham, page 27 © Thinkstock, page 28 © Getty Images/Tier Und Naturfotografie Jund C Sohns, page 29 © Getty Images/Jurgen & Christine Sohns.

The National Wildlife Federation & Ranger Rick contributors: Children's Publication Staff, Licensing Staff including Deana Duffek, Michael Morris & Kristen Ferriere, and the National Wildlife Federation in-house naturalist David Mizejewski

Thank you for joining the National Wildlife Federation and Muddy Boots in preserving endangered animals and protecting vital wildlife habits. The National Wildlife is a voice for wildlife protection, dedicated to preserving America's outdoor traditions and inspiring generations of conservationists.

All rights reserved. No part of this book may be reproduced in any form or by any electronic or mechanical means, including information storage and retrieval systems, without written permission from the publisher, except by a reviewer who may quote passages in a review.

British Library Cataloguing-in-Publication Information available

Library of Congress Control Number: 2016912765

ISBN 978-1-63076-226-1 (paperback)
ISBN 978-1-63076-227-8 (electronic)

The paper used in this publication meets the minimum requirements of American National Standard for Information Sciences—Permanence of Paper for Printed Library Materials, ANSI/NISO Z39.48-1992.

Printed in the United States of America

Contents

Do you like to play?
Animals do, too!

All kinds of animals have
fun playing games
and running wild.

A grizzly bear cub tries to tag his sister.

TAG, YOU'RE IT!

Where do animals
like to hide?
A giraffe calf
hides under Mom.

Animals wrestle to have
fun and grow strong.
Lion cubs tackle each other.

HOPSCOTCH

Mountain goats hop from rock to rock on a mountain top.

A stick can be a fun toy.
A fox kit plays
with a big stick.

Trees are nature's jungle gyms. A brown bear cub climbs a tall tree.

MOM'S TAIL

Sometimes, tails are toys. Lion cub thinks Mom's tail is fun to catch.

17

A tree branch is a fun swing. Little orangutans like to swing upside down.

Dolphins love to leap and splash in the water.

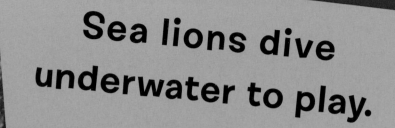

Sea lions dive underwater to play.

SURFING

Penguins surf the waves for fun.

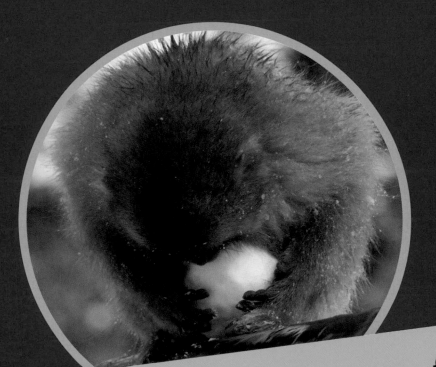

Animals with warm fur coats love snowy days. Japanese snow monkeys make snowballs.

SNOW BALLS

SNOW ANGELS

It looks like a harp seal pup is making snow angels.

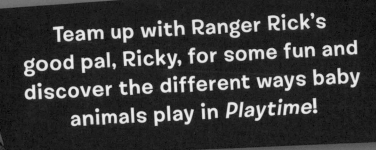

Team up with Ranger Rick's good pal, Ricky, for some fun and discover the different ways baby animals play in *Playtime*!

With adorable full-color photographs throughout and chock-full of interesting animals, Ranger Rick Jr. books are perfect for young children starting to learn about the world around them. These small books are a great way to start your child's first library!

Playtime will explore how animals have fun! Learn about animals around the world through photographs and educational, entertaining text. Just like us, animals have their own ways of playing, and this book will feature many of them in all types of exciting situations!

Thank you for joining Ranger Rick, the National Wildlife Federation, and Muddy Boots in promoting wildlife and conservation education. The National Wildlife Federation's Ranger Rick® magazine has been enjoyed by children and trusted by parents and teachers for more than 50 years. Ranger Rick's new books further educate and engage kids with the natural world around them and inspire future generations of conservationists to explore the great outdoors.

The National Wildlife Federation
©2017 All rights reserved

muddy boots™

we jump in puddles

An imprint of Globe Pequot
MuddyBootsBooks.com
Distributed by
NATIONAL BOOK NETWORK
800-462-6420

$5.99

ISBN 978-1-63076-226-1

9 781630 762261   50599

T3-BCC-913

"I'm doing my best," grunted Bob. Suddenly the plank came loose
and Bob fell back on his bottom.
Things weren't going that well for Bob on his birthday!

Back at the yard Dizzy and Muck watched Wendy make Bob's birthday cake. "Cake mixing looks easy," said Dizzy. "You just throw everything together and mix it up. Just like making concrete!"

"Hey, why don't we make Bob a concrete cake he can keep forever? **Can we make it?**" asked Muck.

"**Yes, we can!**" exclaimed Dizzy.

Dizzy whipped up a load of her very best concrete. Then she poured it into a tire mold.

Then Roley helped Muck and Dizzy decorate their concrete cake with some flowers, feathers, and leaves.

"Wow! Cool cake," Roley said.

At Farmer Pickles's barn Bob and Lofty were still working hard. Their work was coming along nicely.

"Travis and Spud, aren't you two supposed to be delivering Farmer Pickles's eggs?" asked Bob.

"You're right!" said Travis, starting up his engine. "Come on Spud," he called. "I'll drop you off at Bob's house."

At Bob's house Wendy was done making Bob's birthday cake.
"Mmmmmm!" exclaimed Spud, as he scooped some icing off the
cake and plopped it into his mouth.

"Spud!" Wendy yelled.

"I'm sorry, Wendy," Spud mumbled. "But it looks so good!"

"Do you want to help me put the candles on the cake?" asked Wendy.

"You bet! Spud's on the job!" he laughed.

As Bob nailed the last plank into Farmer Pickles's barn, his cell phone rang. "Maybe this is a birthday phone call," he said hopefully. It was Wendy. "Hi, Bob," she said. "When are you coming home?"

"Actually we've just finished and we are on our way," Bob told her.
"Why . . . any special reason?"
"No," Wendy replied. "I've just got a few letters for you to sign. Bye."
"No 'Happy Birthday, Bob'," Bob murmured to himself.
Scoop winked at Lofty. "Come on, Bob. Time to go home!" he said.

Back at the yard Wendy, Muck, Dizzy, and Roley had
decorated a table and covered it with cakes and presents.
Bob couldn't believe his eyes when he arrived back at the yard.

"Surprise!" laughed Wendy.

"I thought you forgot my birthday!" Bob exclaimed.

"Forget your birthday?" Wendy teased. "Never! Look! You've got two cakes—a real cake to eat and a concrete cake you can keep forever!"

Everybody burst out singing:

"Bob the Builder, it's his birthday!
Bob the Builder, yes it is!
It's Bob's birthday, can we sing it?
It's Bob's birthday—yes, we can!"

"And don't forget your mail!" Wendy said.
"All these birthday cards for me?" gasped Bob.
"Of course," replied Wendy, "you're the Birthday Builder!"
Everyone cheered, "Hooray!"

"Now can I please have a slice of that yummy-looking
cake?" begged Spud, interrupting.
"Of course you may," said Bob, as he cut Spud a huge piece.

Spud stuffed the piece of cake into his mouth and smiled.
"Like I always say: 'I'm on the job, Bob!'"